Reflections on Love, Life & Loss

Cover photo: Reshma Mituram

Published by Ixora Press

PO Box 64022, Toronto, ON, M5J 2T6, Canada

Website: www.ixorapress.com

contact@ixorapress.com

ISBN: 978-1-7380363-1-8

For All of My Loved Ones
Past, Present and Future

Table of Contents

LIFE

LOSS

Introduction

When I began writing the poems in this book, it wasn't for the purpose of publishing. It was so that I could make room in my head so that the other projects I've been working on since I was 18 could have a chance. I started putting Reflections of Love, Life and Loss on paper in June 2019 along with another collection, Earth Songs, which I have yet to present to the world.

Throughout my life, I have used poetry as a form of self-therapy during times of emotional turbulence, of pain and frustration at not understanding my place or if I even had a place in this world. It was a way to work through my recurring bouts of existential angst, the likes of which would give even Hamlet a run for his money. I owe my Muses, fickle as they are, a mountain of gratitude.

Love is the first section in this collection because, why not? It pervades all aspects of the human condition so naturally I felt that this section should begin with a confession. The poems I selected to place into the section titled *Life*, are a combination of poems that allude to fear, foreboding, disappointment, hope, guilt and the promise of something better. *The 500* is especially interesting to me since I have no idea what it is meant to be. Perhaps it's a promise that all is not lost even if it seems to be that way. I don't question the words I just write them. It's only after reading and re-reading them can I see what messages lay within and assign an appropriate title. Perhaps you the reader can see something in it that I cannot.

The final section *Loss*, like *Love*, speaks for itself. Who hasn't known it? Who hasn't felt its grip around your throat and its cold hand squeezing your insides as the magnitude of who or what was lost settles over you? It was the section that I wrote during the first couple of months of the pandemic when there was so much loss everywhere. Images of pain, sorrow and desperation have permanently etched themselves into my mind.

It is important to also note that when we think of loss in the context of our lives and relationships, we often neglect to consider that the loss of hope and faith in oneself is just as painful as the loss of a loved one and can often go unnoticed until it is too late and for that purpose *Surrender* was written.

I hope that whoever you are, wherever you are in your life's journey, should you be holding this book at this very moment, may you find the words that you need to be at peace.

Love

Confession

You
Carry my love like a wounded bird
cupped gently in warm hands
severed heartstrings remain unheard
leaving hounds to haunt these lands

You
shed liquid diamonds from the depths
of the pools glittering on your face
for the shattered pieces of my empty self
scattered all over the place

You
wrap my soul like fragile glass
protecting it from my shame
hiding it from deeds of the past
shielding it from blame

You

cradle my heart like a sleeping child
and rock the storm away
soothing that which misery defiled
keeping the pain at bay

You

saved the worrying fool that I am
and sheltered me from devastation
turning my tempests to an even calm
as I crawl towards my salvation.

Everlasting

Dear sweet bird, sing your songs in praise of everlasting love
Share your heart with the wretches below and the stars in heavens above
Ride the wind and spread the word that such a thing does exist
Tell the bards to write the verse to sway those who resist

Come with me, take my hand and step over the threshold
There's so much more on the other side that you'd want to behold
Spread your wings, if wings you have and soar to abundant feeling
Grasp them well in longing hands as they hang from the limitless ceiling

Close your eyes and surrender to this vast, inexplicable joy
of a love that knows no bounds and that which hate seeks to destroy
Come closer now, do not fear the sound of my beating heart
Its rhythm echoes the universe that began humming at the start

Write the odes, write the sonnets and do all else that you will
to praise the love that remains as time and everlasting till
the magic fades into the dark and burns with fallen stars
and Earth rolls over and closes her eyes in the shadow of angry Mars

Oh sweet bird, sing your songs until your time has come
My people and I will float by on the note of the primordial hum
By carrying your song of everlasting love, we can let the healing start
We will protect the magic that has no end and which hate would tear apart.

Apology

Forgive me
for the cuts I made to your soft and wounded heart
Look not upon the face burning with regret
Humbled by your innocence like an unintended dart
I hide my face in shame for the ills I did abet

Forgive me
for the daggers I threw at your unsuspecting back
and the salt that was rubbed on those wounds too
Cowed by your courage against my vicious attack
I surrender my weapons and the evil I do

Forgive me
for the envy that slithered across my mind
and strangled the goodwill that lived there
Leaving in its place a dark hollow for me to find
in which was placed my borrowed fear

Forgive me

if you can and if you cannot I understand

Some wounds go too deep to be healed

I will roll up my follies and wait for the hand

of the justice that would someday be revealed.

Forgiveness

Look at you with your gaze bolted to the ground

There is no joy in the stoop of a back bent forward under the weight of shame

Nor is there satisfaction in knowing that dragons squat upon your head breathing fires of regret into dreams riddled with blame

Step into the light, hold your head high and let fall from your neck the lodestone carved out of guilt

Throw off the shroud that was woven from the strands of all the moments you spent locked in that cage you built

Hush now, say no more about your reckless darts

What was said and done has come and gone and mercy longs to visit

Go forth into the light taking measured steps towards the fire of absolution

There now, be free, live again as forgiveness warms your spirit.

Tribal

One body, one blood, one soul
fused together to make one whole
eyes recognize the likeness of others
the same fruit borne from different mothers

One hope, one dream, one desire
hearts burn in a restless fire
which began when freedom was taken
leaving them bound, forgotten and forsaken

One battle, one struggle, one war
time rushes on with a deafening roar
the battered and broken left in its wake
no prisoners left and no dignity to take

One heart, one mind, one kind
look within to seek and to find
that which binds the world as one
a Universal tribe under one sun.

The Kindness of Strangers

Faceless amongst moving pieces on an infinite board
Aimless and drifting closer to the edge of the sword
that beheads purpose and slays every reason for living
in a world where love is at war with the unforgiving

Tendrils of goodwill reach out in search of endless pain
from the ones who have fallen, unable to rise again
then appearing as if by magic to apply a soothing balm
to wounds dealt by a life made of storms without calm

Never ones to linger in the hopes of receiving praise
they press on through the masses and are lost in the human maze
never to be seen again except in a random glance,
a trickery of the mind or simply pure happenstance

Wherever do they go after pulling us from the brink
of tumbling into despair, of severing that vital link
between the conditions that make us human, that lend us strength to cope
and the frenzied race for power and supremacy without hope?

They're hidden somewhere in the crush of drifting humanity

with eyes peeled for sorrow and suffering, hearts primed to see

those of us who are lost and seem broken beyond repair

these strangers armed with their kindness, will defend you with care.

Lullaby

Be still,
let it wash over you and drown out the cruel voices
let it roar, let it rumble
singing loudly, let it tumble
off the cliffs of regretted choices

Raise your head, dry your eyes
hear the thunder on distant skies
like drums of a percussion band

Listen well, listen true
for the voices to start on cue
reverberating across the land

Hum the tune, mark the beat
keeping time with mindless feet
while sleep hovers high above

Pull the blanket, drift away
the night has claimed another day
wrapping life in the arms of love.

This Promise

Like candlelight flickering in weighty darkness
and incense wafting through the air
a hint of sanity shining through madness
as thunderclouds begin to clear

Like eagle wings glinting in the sun
and raindrops quenching parched earth
myriad hearts will beat as one
as our embattled mother again gives birth

Like a diamond dew drop on glistening grass
heralding a newborn day
a golden dawn turning water to glass
while creatures kneel to pray

Like white water caressing a lonely shore
while formidable cliffs look on
and fishermen hold the line till they are sore
as red stains the vast horizon

Like the fragrance of flowers in bloom
and their colours that gladden opened eyes
chasing away the spectre of doom
as tears fall from angry skies

Like the crescendo of a sweet symphony
that drowns the pain of sorrow
declaring the arrival of destiny
who will come riding in tomorrow.

My Brother, My Friend

Walk with me a little
to the edge of forever
Break not the ties
that bind us together
Stay a while my brother
take my hand my friend
Let us watch the time pass
till we are at the end.

Sister

So not like me
yet so much like me
I knew you when you were young
I see you even now
How time has flown
on wings made of imaginary adventures

Let us again step through the portal
in the small coconut tree
and into our realm for a serving of tea
Then onwards to mountains that yearn for the skies
and fountains of youth in the depths of our eyes
fighting demons and ghouls in our righteous war
guarding the realm in our childhood lore

Each sunrise was counted, and each sunset admired
while chance and destiny cruelly conspired
to lead us into battles we had no chance of winning
restrained as we were with the webs they kept spinning
and yet there we were in world of our creation
relentless and defiant in our quest for liberation

With fear firmly tucked in the palms of our hands
we set out to discover the shores of other lands
some day in our hearts we will finally conquer
the longing that burns both brighter and stronger
while dreaming of the day when the whole world will see
how much I am like you and why you are just like me.

The Brotherhood

Speak not of what sets us apart
see only with the eyes that peer from the heart
this is not the end.

Walk with me for a little while
step for step, mile for mile
till darkness begins to descend

We could recall all those memories
of a time before this heavy unease
that none can comprehend

Look how silently time flies by
how truth is savaged by a lie
that the flawed cannot ascend

Lift your head, own your place
bless the world with your hidden grace
allow what has been broken to mend

Farewells will come again once more
you will leave through that door
and disappear around the bend

Have no fear, we will wait
right here at this open gate
till your guilt and fury are spent.

The Silent Hero

He waits silently on the edge of all awareness
scanning the horizon for the signs of a kinder tomorrow
A hero's badge he wears, tucked away in the warmth of his heart
hidden, where no one can see while he waits for his time to come
Words longing for life remain unspoken
lest they be drowned in an ocean of silence
too vast, too dark and too deep
for his love to be heard.

Mother

Little one, take my hand, the road is long and winding

I will lead the way past obstacles and through visions that are spell binding

Treachery lurks at each turn and bend but so can happiness too

Their names you will learn before the end, which ones are false or true

I will pick you up after each fall until you can do so on your own

When you stand your ground before temptation, I will know that you've truly grown

The time will come for you to carry on without me right by your side

Just as dusk always precedes the dawn, by these rules I must abide

Little one, take hold of my hand and hold on for dear life

I will guide you along the pathways filled with unexpected strife

Stay the course and trust your heart but enjoy the beauty too

Make your mark so *your* little one can follow just like you do

For just like me you will have to make that unimaginable journey

To a place that lies beyond all reason and no one will ever see.

The Secret Love of Pets

What are you thinking when you look at me?

Is there something that you know? Something you see?

Do I fill you with joy when I walk into the room?

Does my voice dispel the silence, the boredom and the gloom?

I wonder at your thoughts when you sit and stare at me

Am I everything you hoped that your life would be?

When you brush against my knee or stick your head under my arm

Does my warm and gentle hug keep you happy, keep you calm?

And those presents that you bring from who knows where

Is this your way of saying just how much you really care?

Do you feel it when the end is creeping quickly upon you?

And would you still love me when I don't know what else to do?

It is so unfair that I should muddle on for so long

But your little beating heart must soon end its loving song

You are my precious gem and the apple of each eye

I'll hold on to your love even after you say goodbye.

Coming Home

Footprints along the path where others trod before
lead me at long last to that familiar door
Now open in warm welcome, inviting me inside
to a loving embrace and a safe place to hide
from a world full of troubles and a creeping loss of faith
in those we choose to lead us from the brink of endless hate
Resting in the presence of the ones who have my love
in a home under the stars that hang so high above
I hold my hope before me, like an orb of the purest light for
kinder tomorrows when we no longer have to fight.

Life

Echo

I hear voices
that bounce off the resilience
of time and space
echoing above and below
and around, reciting the laws
of humanity and drowning
the hum of a universe
that scowls with disdain
at our fragility and delusion
that this is ours
ALL OF IT
created for us
to use as we please
until it cracks and crumbles
piercing the bubble
that protects the ultimate
LIE.

Rhythm

All hail the emperor who rests on a throne
Ruling over flesh, over blood and fragile bone
Pushing the beat of life and chaotic existence
Riding the unseen waves, destroying all resistance

Come cheer the Commander, fighting a raging war
Against the silence of a beat deafening law
In time with the pulsing of every precious heart
Erasing the differences that rip peace apart

Who rocks the soul of every living tribe and
excites the blood beyond what one can describe?

Who burrows deep down into every moving cell
and quickens the heart when the crescendo begins to swell?

Who rolls with the sea and rocks with the land
and lives within the sound of each cosmic band?

Go tell everyone who will lend an attentive ear

The beat of your drums could never compare

To the rhythm of life in all its magnificence

And its power to drown out our loud insignificance.

The 500

They rest upon beds of lost yesterdays
Curled up under covers of destinies
Eyelids twitch on dreams of loving rays
While the General weaves seconds into stories
The Watchers, they gather in the long, ominous shadows
Of past deeds that were bloody and bold
On guard to guide the slumbering hallows
Through a future that is cruel and cold
Light pierces the core of enveloping darkness
Like a beacon that blinks from afar
Exposing the lingering, soul crushing harshness
That creeps through the door left ajar
Egos have swollen like foul, black waters
And rush on like a thundering flood
Gouging the wombs of their defiant daughters
While their sons forge weapons from blood
Silence rings a death deafening alarm
A warning the 500 will arise

The deluge of poison slows to a calm
As the soldiers begin opening their eyes
Today we shall sweep the ashes away
of a long and red, turbulent past
The hundreds are here at the dawn of the day
To lead the willing blind at long last
Onwards they march to their waiting posts
Towards what humanity hath forsaken
Long banners flutter in the eyes of the hosts
For Time has won and the Herald is awakened.

The Guardians

Like a whisper in the wind
Trailing dew drops on my skin
Spinning magic in the night
From strands of russet twilight
Fill the air with soulful song
Tip the pot of gold at dawn
Blow the ripples on the ocean
Set the hurricanes in motion
Paint the world in vibrant hues
Wash the sky with gentle blues
Tame the roar of hungry surf
Splash with green the blackened turf
Lift the wings of feathered friends
Till the silver lady ascends
Write the rules of time and space
While the players earn their grace

In the end we make our beds

Upon which we must lay our heads

To dream of yet another life

Free of pain and needless strife.

Sigma

Oh Andromeda, where have you hidden her
The new jewel of this roiling Universe?
She whose life will sow seeds of hope
Once Terra is abandoned and forgotten
Fetch her from behind the swirls
of her sister's beauty and brilliance
Uncover her shy face
so that all may gaze upon her grace
Unseen is she to the eyes of seekers
who would scan infinity in search of a new abode
Andromeda, present your debutante
Shield her not from new admirers
Pray, let her step into the light
So that she may witness how the wretched horde
has finally come to heel.

The Warriors

Leave us not without our armour which encases our heartfelt pride

Drain us not of our fervour and the purpose for which we ride

Hold aloft the gold standards of the blameless leaders we follow

Trailing the fearless vanguard and making whole what was once hollow

Seek and destroy wily foes who threaten our sovereign lands

Leaving them in the throes of the pain dealt with our hands

For strangers are no real threat if we strike at them before

Turn their lives to sudden death so they can frighten us no more

Look here, all around us now, how our follies have been scattered

In victorious pride we take a bow as if humanity never mattered

Tomorrow we'll grace the reddened ground with wreaths of proud regret

To mark the days with solemn sound and remind those who would dare forget

Warriors today are tomorrow's dead and Kings and Tyrants will fall

A battleground becomes a bed when the grinning shadow comes to call

No righteous might or grim foresight can shroud us from its gaze

We smile beneath self-inflicted blight and thus we end our days.

The Light

Look not at this face hidden beneath a veil of disgrace
Avert the orbs that will pass judgment without cause
Dwell not upon the wounds that widen with each blow
Thus, marking the wearer with tattoos of discontent
Go deeper than you have ever gone
Plumb the depths of the unknown
Where your fear rests in a fetid pool
You cannot see the light that evades your common gaze
You will not see the light that caresses the eyes of those
who proudly wear their battle scars
Trophies, they are, of wars lost and won.

Untitled

And so we wait…
till an unknown mother claims the fruit of her womb
Orphans of broken galaxies, we stumble through each cycle
mouths agape, eyes and ears shut
taking everything, giving nothing back
twisted at our very core
spiraling down past the foundations
upon which was built the great miracle
that we were supposed to be
though not as eagerly as those who came and went before
leaving chasms gouged into destinies
too far off to see.

Chaos

Quicker than a flash of lightning
all in the blink of an eye
at a speed that is utterly frightening
truth succumbs to a rotten lie

Cracks widen in weak foundations
driving deeper and further apart
wrenching the souls from dying nations
while rot creeps into each heart

Houses of glass perch on the brink
of chasms devoid of reason
and those who cast rocks fail to think
their actions reek of high treason

For when Ego slithers from its cave
the sun and sky will fall
crushing each self-seeking knave
and raining chaos upon us all.

Pandemonium

Calamity stands before the golden gates
intent on shaking ivory towers into dust
The righteous unmask the terror that awaits
so the weak and the weary can flee if they must
Peace gasps under the weight of discontent
carried by those who were broken and bled
See the revolution of which many have dreamt
before the bell tolls for the uncounted dead.

Demons

There in the corner, where no other eyes can see
reposed on a bed of doubts, staring straight at me
Resplendent in robes woven from my guilt
you make your abode in this world I have built
Forever at my heels, leaning heavily against my back
filling my mind with all the virtues that I lack
Hiding all that is good beneath billowing, acrid smoke
feeding me the lies upon which I slowly choke
Your voices drip like poison into an innocent ear
while your fingers beckon chaos, misery and fear
Together you make this life a wretched, living hell
torturing my spirit, killing the will to rebel
Cowards you are who go lurking in the shadows
for the weak and the willful whose contempt steadily grows
Where has my hope gone, wherefore does it hide
while love is being stifled and goodwill has died?
It's locked in a corner, where only you can see
Waiting for the moment you finally set it free.

Burning Bridges

There is no return to what was once before
Smoke and embers declare the deed is done
Onwards to tomorrow now that yesterday is gone
I revel in the peace that the others abhor.

Promises

So it has begun…

counting the days till we get all that was promised

in return for our loyalty

scanning black and white horizons for signs,

any sign of reprieve from a life that weighs heavily

on limbs weakened by the grasp of the collector's far-reaching hands

Nights greet us huddled together in hope, with bellies full of promises

as we await the arrival of noble sleep who grants us mercy

so we may dream of a dawn that frees us from our purgatory.

Loss

Remembering Yesterday

Surrender

As I Am

Skeletons

Shattered

Regret

The Bridge

Farewell

The Collector

Remembering Yesterday

Looking back to the days before
when nothing made much sense
The past is gone forevermore
and today abhors our presence
Blood and sweat hath watered the ground
and tears did fall there too
Silent souls still wander around
in fear of what we will do
Golden legacies of yesterday
lay smothered in cold ashes
The present world is in disarray
as the future secretly watches.

Surrender

Fingers grip the edge above the dark as despair tugs at my feet, urging me down

The stars above huddle together for solace, blinking in disbelief at my weakness and determination to slip into this unknown

How did I get here?

Before me, the fence wobbles on its pikes burdened by the weight of my dejection

Time is not welcome here

Seconds pass by uncounted and uninterested while light slipped away unnoticed

The deep beckons, cajoles, dares me to resist the stubborn urge to clamber onto the fence where I once perched and pondered the ultimate surrender of my soul in return for limitless peace.

As I Am

See the blemishes that adorn my skin
marked for life by unforgotten sin
Through the cracks you can see my soul
falling to pieces from what was whole
From the dark, my defiant will crept
and stole past guards who soundly slept
Drunk on sweet, power spiced wine
laced with lies from a proxy divine
Blood-tinged eyes peer at distant shores
and upon them rests wide, open doors
through which I would pass but cannot reach
thus reprieve denied on a sinking beach
Alone and forlorn my soul cries out
against a wrenching roundabout
of misplaced hopes and stolen dreams
with no end in sight and for what seems
an eternity that went, another to come
with torment for me and heaven for some

Mark the place where I stood my ground
counting the blows without making a sound
as these bones now have turned to steel
and with this armour I no longer feel
the weight of judgment crashing down on me
and the loss of who I once longed to be.

Skeletons

Locked away from cold, prying eyes for fear of humiliation

in the place where dignity dies under the weight of retribution

No bitter tears can wash away the stench of denigration

and no heartfelt pleas can thus delay an inevitable annihilation

These ravaged bones can testify to a life of aggravation

in this underworld that we glorify whose demagogues deliver devastation

Peeking through the rusty keyhole in futile search of liberation

and finding naught but a withered soul on the brink of self damnation

Waiting for the world to witness the reverse of human evolution

in times when logic is amiss and lies feed paranoid revolution

Own the darkness, rest here in peace and seek no fragile validation

the time will come for life to cease and reckon with Her retaliation.

Shattered

Glass, at the mercy of relentless gravity
scattered about in a million shards of clarity

Sheets of ice, with the first breath of spring
when the winter breeze has lost its brutal sting

A heart, at the point of a careless dart
beats one last beat before it is torn apart

Tears, that fall as acid rain
for the ones who were lost, will never be seen again.

Regret

Is,

Like choking down a piece of stale bread
unable to breathe, blinded by tears
Like blood heavy with lead
coursing through me, feeding my fears
Like shackles that bind my feet
grinding bone to dust, crushing me in its hold
Like my conscience being dragged beneath
an infinite ocean of misery untold.

The Bridge

Meet me on the bridge
in between now and soon forever
where the light touches the dark
and two worlds come together

Meet me on the bridge
between the moments we have shared
drawing them out as long as we could
hoping that we will be spared

Meet me on the bridge
in between your first and final smile
on knowing that your journey's beginning and end
might only last a little while

Meet me on the bridge
in that space between our skin
where our hands are clutched in desperate denial
that the end will soon begin

Meet me on the bridge
between the sound of your last sigh
where your breath mingles with mine
and your new journey is nigh

Meet me on the bridge
in between the beats of your loyal heart
as they fade away into the distance
and our worlds grow further apart

Meet me on the bridge
in between the place where hope remains
and where sorrow finds a loving hand
to help soothe the coming pains

Meet me on the bridge
before you go for one last embrace
as time is closing in on us
and stealing our space

Meet me on the bridge, dear one
where our love will forever abide
please, stay just a little longer with me
before you cross to the other side.

Farewell

Tomorrow should never come if you walk away today
Must I will the moments to stand still until
there is nothing else left to say?

The road unknown lies ahead and awaiting your travels
Would you allow me a place by your side
before your promise truly unravels?

No blow will break me like the one you have dealt
Must I now stop my heart, cut it out
and deny everything I have felt?

Now you must turn away and head off on your journey
leaving me, waiting right here, hoping
that you will choose to come back for me.

The Collector

There is nowhere to run and nowhere to hide
Rules are rules and by them you will abide
Turn out those pockets, hold out your covered palms
Dues must be paid; I care not for meagre alms
No tears can sway me, this ploy I've seen before
My will has no end even before a padlocked door
Hand over all of that which you must give
This is the price for all who would live
No path stays open, no passage beyond is free
To cross into new land will cost you a fee
Speak no words of flattery, they fall on deaf ears
Honeyed words have no effect when your account is in arrears
All that you have ever won is no business of mine
Now hold your head high and join the never-ending line.

Acknowledgments

To my sisters Marsha and Michelle and my mum Rajdaye, thank you for believing that I could even when I convinced myself that I couldn't. Thank you for the hard discussions, the tough love and often gentle reminders that you will always have my back. Thank you for the constant encouragement to take this step forward when the easiest thing to do is to stay hidden.

Thank you to the teachers, friends and many well-wishers of the past and present. I am forever grateful for the part you played in my life for however long you were meant to be in it.

About The Author

RESHMA MITURAM was born and raised in Trinidad, which is one of the islands that make up the twin island nation of Trinidad and Tobago. On January 15, 2007, she emigrated to Canada as a Permanent Resident because she found that she had outgrown life on an island and needed more space to grow and flourish. Reflections on Love, Life and Loss is the first collection to be published. She is a voracious reader and hopes to write and publish the sort of books that made her want to become an author.

www.ingramcontent.com/pod-product-compliance
Lightning Source LLC
LaVergne TN
LVHW010121170826
845678LV00012B/2524

* 9 7 8 1 7 3 8 0 3 6 3 1 8 *